TIME
WHEN

Nicolas Brasch   **Russell Tate**

NELSON
CENGAGE Learning™

Australia • Brazil • Japan • Korea • Mexico • Singapore • Spain • United Kingdom • United States

NELSON
CENGAGE Learning™

Time Travel: When in Rome

Text: Nicolas Brasch
Illustrations: Russell Tate
Editors: Emma Short and Ben Haskin
Design: James Lowe
Series design: James Lowe
Production controller: Lisa Porter
Reprint: Siew Han Ong

Fast Forward Independent Texts
Level 13

ISBN 978 0 17 017943 0
ISBN 978 0 17 017897 6 (set)

Cengage Learning Australia
Level 7, 80 Dorcas Street
South Melbourne, Victoria Australia 3205
Phone: 1300 790 853

Cengage Learning New Zealand
Unit 4B Rosedale Office Park
331 Rosedale Road, Albany, North Shore NZ 0632
Phone: 0508 635 766

For learning solutions, visit **cengage.com.au**

Printed in China by 1010 Printing International Ltd
2 3 4 5 6 7 15

TIME TRAVEL: WHEN IN ROME

Nicolas Brasch   **Russell Tate**

Contents

Chapter 1	The Rainy Day		4
Chapter 2	The New Gladiators		10
Chapter 3	The Last Adventure?		14
Chapter 4	The Fight		18
Chapter 5	The Best Gladiators		22

The Rainy Day

Georgia and Charlie had a time machine.
It was inside an old tree
at the bottom of their garden.

One day,
Georgia and Charlie were sitting inside.
It was raining outside.

"Maybe we should play a game,"
said Charlie.

"I don't want to play a game,"
Georgia told Charlie.
"Let's go on an adventure!"

Georgia ran out the back door
down to the old tree.

Charlie followed Georgia.
Part of him did not want to go
on an adventure.
But another part of him did.

When they got to the tree,
Charlie and Georgia stepped inside.
There were two buttons in the tree.
One was green.
The other was red.

Georgia pressed the green button.
The tree started spinning.

CHAPTER 2

The New Gladiators

When the tree stopped spinning,
Georgia and Charlie stepped out.

They found themselves
in a crowd of people,
who were wearing clothes
that looked like sheets.

The people were all heading towards a large old building in the distance.

Georgia and Charlie were in ancient Rome!

They followed the crowd of people.

Two soldiers walked up to Georgia and Charlie.

"You must be the new gladiators," one of the men said.

"What's a gladiator?" asked Charlie.

The soldiers just laughed.

The soldiers pushed the
children together.
Then they took Georgia and Charlie
to the arena.

CHAPTER 3

The Last Adventure?

The two soldiers put Georgia and Charlie in the middle of the arena.
A big crowd stared at them.

The soldiers gave helmets
to Georgia and Charlie.
Georgia was given a net.
Charlie was given a sword.
Then the soldiers left them.

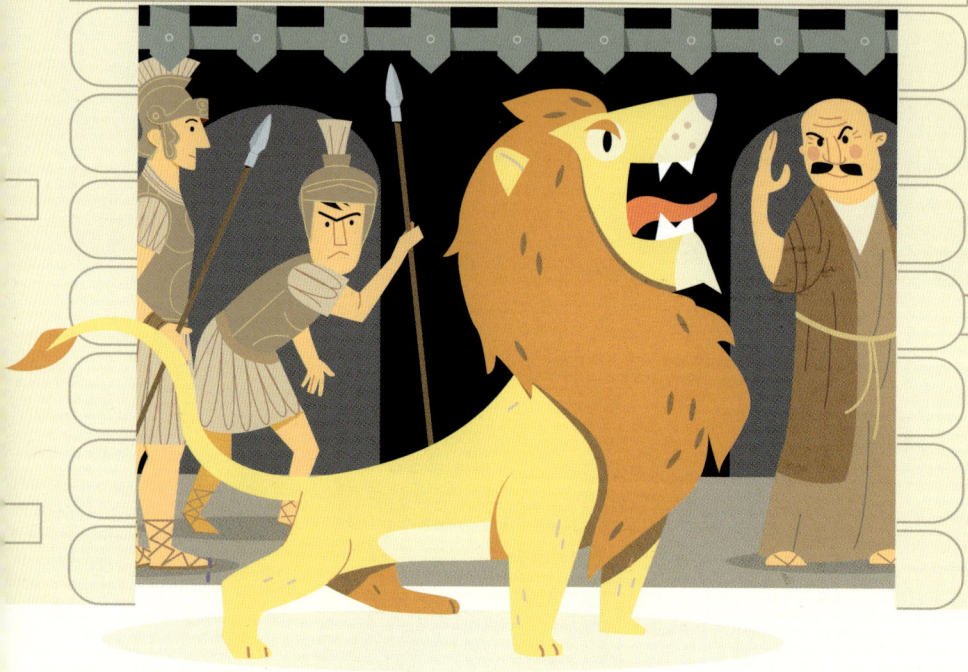

Georgia and Charlie heard a noise
behind them.
They turned and looked,
but they could not believe their eyes.

A big lion had walked
into the arena!

16

The lion roared loudly,
then it started running towards them.

"This could be our very last adventure,"
Charlie cried.

CHAPTER 4

The Fight

"When the lion gets close,
run behind it," Georgia shouted.

She held the net in front of her.

"It *is* close," Charlie screamed.

"Let it get closer," shouted Georgia.

The lion got closer.

"Now?" asked Charlie.

"Not yet," shouted Georgia.

The lion got even closer.

"NOW!" shouted Georgia.

Charlie ran behind the lion.

"Now hit its tail with your sword," Georgia shouted.

"It will kill me," screamed Charlie.

"Just do it!" roared Georgia.

Charlie hit the lion's tail.

The lion turned and roared at Charlie.

Georgia put the net over it.

The lion was trapped.

CHAPTER 5

The Best Gladiators

Some of the crowd ran
into the middle of the arena.
They picked up Georgia and Charlie.

"You are the best gladiators
we have ever seen!" someone said.

"I can't wait to see your next fight!"
said someone else.

Georgia and Charlie dropped
their helmets.
They jumped to the ground,
and ran as fast as they could.

They ran to the old tree,
and stepped inside the trunk.

"That was a great adventure!"
said Georgia.
She pushed the red button.
Charlie did not say a thing.